Other books by John Patterson include:

A Guide For Enjoying Your Travel Trailer

Growing Older On Two Wheels

Simple Home Brewing

Your Guide to Purchasing a Travel Trailer

John M Patterson

Copyright © 2019 by John M Patterson

All rights reserved

1st Edition 2019

"Thousands of tired, nerve-shaken, over-civilized people are beginning to find out that going to the mountains is going home; that wildness is a necessity"
—John Muir

Table of Contents

Foreword

Chapter 1: Intro to Travel Trailers

Chapter 2 – The Common Travel Trailer Myths

Chapter 3 - Determine Your Needs.

Chapter 4 – Determining your Tow Vehicles Capabilities

Chapter 5 – Selecting a Manufacturer

Chapter 6 - Selecting a Dealership

Chapter 7 – What The Dealership Won't Tell You

Chapter 8 - Getting an Independent Inspection

Chapter 9 - What Is A Walk-Through?

Chapter 10 – When To Sign On The Dotted Line

Chapter 11 – Knowing What Steps I Need To Perform

Chapter 12 – What Are The Essentials For Getting On The Road

Chapter 13 - Creating A Warranty Punch List

Chapter 14 - Beyond The Basics, What Is Needed

Chapter 15 – Creating A Check List

Chapter 16 - What Is A Shakedown Trip?

Chapter 17 - When Problems Arise/Warranty And Otherwise

Chapter 18 - Maintenance And Common Travel Trailer Issues

Chapter 19 - Is it worth the effort

Our Travel Trailers Throughout The Years

Foreword

There are many different ways that people come to a decision to purchase a Travel Trailer. Our journey began after a string of below freezing nights while tent camping in upper Michigan. Since we had two small children at the time, we wanted Mother Nature to have less of an impact on our camping experience.

Our first stop was a large RV dealership very close to our home. After looking at a number of older used travel trailers, we settled on a 1971 Jayco JayWren. This Jayco was sixteen feet long. The couch and table would fold down to form beds. It had a small refrigerator, cooktop, sink, and furnace. The only thing it was missing was a bathroom. Having always been tent campers, not having a bathroom would be fine; we were already used to that. After all, this was an experiment to see if we would enjoy camping in a travel trailer as much as camping in a tent. As long as it had the fundamentals like a furnace and refrigerator, we would be happy.

Since the JayWren was already 18 years old it would need some work. It needed new tires, curtains, and new dinette cushions. Overall it was a nice solid trailer so we bought it. It looked like the days of freezing in a tent were over.

Over the next few weeks I spent my spare time changing tires, wheel bearings, and painting the exterior of the trailer. Meanwhile, Tammy worked on renovating the inside of the camper. Then it was finally time to take the JayWren on its maiden voyage so we could see how we liked that type of travel.

After a week-long journey in South Dakota's Black Hills we knew that the experiment had been a success. This was so much better than setting up a tent and screen room; not to mention having a place to cook and eat (and a furnace). I loved the fact that I was no longer packing up wet tents and tarps. In addition we were no longer waking up with damp clothing.

Although we loved the JayWren we quickly realized we needed a bathroom. So a year later we upgraded to a 1990 Sprinter Travel Trailer with a nice bathroom and bunk beds for the kids. Our local RV Dealership gave us exactly what we paid for the JayWren when we traded it in. That was thirty years ago.

There are many more considerations in buying a travel trailer today because the technology has changed so much.

To consider purchasing a Travel Trailer or any RV for that matter it makes sense to investigate everything about the brand you are considering. There are hundreds of different floor plans and many different manufacturers. There are also many horror stories that revolve around making the wrong decision when purchasing an RV.

We hope that this book serves as a guide so you can think through all of your needs prior to purchasing your travel trailer. There are many more considerations to purchasing a travel trailer than the initial purchase price. Getting a great deal is fine, but later being frustrated and disappointed due to quality or service issues will not feel very satisfying.

When you begin your search you will quickly realize the number of travel trailers is overwhelming. We want to make sure that you are fully armed with the information you need. We have been camping in travel trailers for over 30 years now. We have enjoyed every travel trailer we have owned and only traded for newer models because our personal lifestyle had changed. One thing you need to make sure of as you start your journey is that the trailer you choose meets all of your needs. A trailer that lacks your most important requirements will leave you wondering why you didn't spend more time shopping.

Chapter 1: Intro to Travel Trailers

We live in a nation full of people that love to camp. With so many options available in the RV market place, it may surprise you that Travel Trailers have the number one spot in popularity. In fact, there are More Travel Trailers manufactured than any other style of recreational vehicle. There are over five times as many travel trailers produced than fifth wheel trailers, and the balance of campers produced (Folding Camper Trailers, Truck campers, and Motor Home Types – Class A, B, and C) make up a very small percentage of campers sold.

The selection of Travel Trailers is unbelievably large; everything from Teardrop Camper size to over 40 foot long Trailers are available. So what makes Travel Trailers so popular? This is a hard question to answer, but maybe in part it is due to the flexibility in tow vehicles depending on the weight of the trailer. From large cars, SUV's, or pickup trucks, almost anyone can find a towable that will work. Many travel trailers can now be towed by V6 engines.

More than just saving money on lodging, traveling the highways of America is an adventure.

You never know what you may find on your journey; and the convenience of pulling off at rest stops or a small town for lunch in your own trailer (in particular with small children) is a big benefit. In fact a recent study found that Travel Trailer vacations cost less than other forms of vacation travel even after factoring in fuel prices and the cost of the RV. This study found a savings of anywhere from 34 to 53 percent for travel trailer owners

There is a travel trailer for every budget, and just about every tow vehicle.

In this book we will try to break down all the different aspects to purchasing, maintaining, and camping in a travel trailer. Travel Trailers are not for everyone, and we hope to give you a balanced perspective so you can decide if this type of lifestyle is right for you.

Chapter 2 – The Common Travel Trailer Myths

Prior to buying a Travel Trailer keep in mind that there are quite a few myths or misconceptions that revolve around the purchase and maintenance of Recreational Vehicles. It's very easy to fall under the spell of the dealership as you look at new trailers but it is very important to have your eyes wide open before making a major purchase on a travel trailer. So here are a few of the common travel trailer myths, many points we will delve into a little later on in this book.

My Dealership won't let me purchase an RV that I am unable to tow with my current vehicle. False – The Dealership is trying to sell you an RV. Most of the folks selling the RVs do not know how much your vehicle can tow. This is something you need to know before buying an RV. You need to know your Payload, Axle Gearing, and engine size (just to name a few). Once you have these you can make an informed decision.

A new Travel Trailer will have no issues. False – Travel Trailers are not built by robots (like automobiles). The RV industry builds trailers by hand. It is unrealistic to think that a new travel trailer will not have some issues. This is why we recommend using it often during the warranty period. You may hear folks on-line refer to a "Shake Down Trip". They are talking about discovering (shaking out) all the issues with a new trailer.

If I buy a New Travel Trailer I don't need to have it inspected. False – Years ago this might have been true – but not anymore. This is a huge investment, so before you sign any paperwork please have your unit independently inspected. The inspection process provided by an independent inspector will be much more in depth than your dealership. The cost of an independent inspection is relatively inexpensive, given the purchase price of an RV. This will help you minimize issues from #2 above.

I can tow without any special hitch for my Travel Trailer. False – You will need a weight distribution hitch. The hitch needs to be rated for the weight of the trailer you plan on towing. To tow without weight distribution is endangering yourself and others.

All Travel Trailers are manufactured exactly the same. False – While the manufacturing processes are similar, the materials that are used vary from manufacturer to manufacturer. So before you buy, do your research on how the frame and walls are constructed; and how well the manufacturer stands behind their product. Almost everything you need to know about a manufacturer's process can be found on the internet.

My Travel Trailer is like a car, the warranty covers everything during the warranty period. False – You are responsible for many parts of the trailer during the warranty period. Case in point: It is your responsibility to periodically inspect the roof to make sure that there are no voids in the sealant. If you find voids, you will need to apply sealant or have your dealership perform this repair. Not taking care of your RV may void the warranty.

Most RV campgrounds are horrible and over-crowded. False – While there are always campgrounds that are sub-standard there are many other campgrounds that are beautiful. Always look online and at reviews in order to minimize a disappointing camping trip.

The only good RV is a "insert type of RV here". False – Whether it is a Travel Trailer, Fifth Wheel, Class A, etc., base your purchase on only one thing: Does it fit the needs of what you and your family require. That is the most important prerequisite. If you don't follow this rule you will probably be purchasing another RV really soon.

Travel Trailers can't have a residential appearance on the inside. False – While there was probably some truth to this claim years ago, it certainly isn't true anymore. Many RVs look like small houses on the inside with residential cabinetry, furnishings, and all the amenities. Almost all have Microwaves, Ovens, flat screen TVs, Cable Hook ups, Large Bathrooms etc. There is a reason some folks refer to it as Glamping (not Camping).

Travel Trailers are extremely expensive. False – Travel Trailers have a wide range of pricing based on size and amenities. If you want to save a lot of money then look for a used model and save on all the depreciation you will experience buying new. In addition, buying a used model may have the advantage that all of the "bugs" have been worked out. An independent inspection on a used unit is also a good idea.

Camping in Travel Trailers is only for retired folks. False – A typical travel trailer owner is 49 years old. In fact, more RVs are owned by people between the ages of 35 to 54 than any other age group. The population of young people camping is growing every year.

It is Cheaper to just stay in a Hotel than to travel in an RV. False – In fact a recent study found that Travel Trailer vacations cost less than other forms of vacation travel even after factoring in fuel prices and the cost of the RV. This study found a savings of anywhere from 34 to 53 percent for travel trailer owners.

Hopefully these points will help dispel a few of the common travel trailer myths that exist. Having a travel trailer can be a wonderful experience. Like everything else in life; plenty of information always leads to better decision making.

Chapter 3 - Determine Your Needs.

At this point we will assume that you have made a decision to, at the very least, investigate what camping would be like in a Travel Trailer. Our decision to look at travel trailers was driven by a couple of below freezing nights camping in a tent with our small children. It was June in northern Michigan near Mackinac Island, and we never expected that kind of weather. It became apparent as we left the tent for a hotel room that something had to change. Tent camping had been great up to this point but it just wasn't optimal for our family anymore. I was tired of using a tent heater and waking up with moisture over everything and huddling next to a campfire with small children.

Now that we had made a conscious decision to move to a different mode of camping we had to decide what would best meet the needs of our family.

We have been through this process eight times now so hopefully what we have learned will be of benefit to you in your search for the perfect home away from home.

The following is a list of things to consider as you ponder what Travel Trailer might be right for you:

Overall Construction

Do not assume that all travel trailers are constructed the same way. Research the models you are interested in and understand how they differ from each other in their construction. For example, is the floor made from a wood frame. Or is it metal construction? How is the roof constructed; and how much weight can it support? Most manufacturers will have a page on their website that talks about their specific construction process. Don't forget to research their warranty and find out what others are saying about their product(s).

Sleeping Quarters

- Bed(s) – Bed's come in many different sizes in RV's, don't assume that a Queen size is always a Queen size; there are standard (like in your house) and then there are Short Queens which are not as long. Take time to lay down on the bed and make sure it will work for you. Also make sure the mattress is a decent quality; so you won't be forced to replace it after a few nights of painful sleep.

- Windows – Is cross ventilation important to you? Will you spend nights with the windows open? Then you need to make sure that there is adequate cross ventilation. Don't assume that all the windows you see throughout your trailer will open. Some windows are emergency exits and may not function like a regular window. In addition, don't assume that all the windows will open fully. Many windows today do not open as wide as you might imagine.
- Accessibility – Can you move around in the bedroom easily (plenty of room around the bed)? Can you make the bed without being a contortionist? Is there enough space that you can easily reach into the back of cabinets and closets? In many bedrooms there are built in nightstands that may make it difficult to reach to the rear of the closet or the overhead cabinets. If there is storage under the bed can you easily open and remove items without hitting the walls?

- Closets – Is there enough space for your clothes, and do the clothes hang easily in the closet without folding over on the compartment floor?
- Nightstand – Is there enough room on the nightstand for your phone, books, computer, a fan? Are there enough electrical plugs on or near the nightstand so you can charge your personal electronics as you sleep?
- Outlets – Does the room have enough outlets for all your needs? If you wanted to put a nightlight on the floor, would you have any options for where it would go? If you wanted to plug-in a fan, would that be possible?
- Lighting – Are the lights easy enough to turn off when you go to bed? Are any reading lights over the bed going to prevent your partner from sleeping if you want to read?
- Television – Does the unit come with a TV or would you need to have one installed? Some RV's can share a TV with the living area (It swivels). If you need to add a TV to the bedroom, then determine if that has an impact on your ability to move about the bedroom freely.

Living Quarters

- Overall Space Requirements – How many people will be sleeping in the trailer? Are there enough sofa sleepers or tables that drop down into sleepers to accommodate your family. When all the beds are extended can you still move around in the trailer? Is the table/booth large enough to accommodate your family during meals? Can you get into the bumped out areas (such as the table) without hitting your head? Is it comfortable to move around in the trailer when everyone is inside, or is it cramped? Does the seating in the living area make sense (i.e. can you watch television and/or talk to others without sitting on a strange angle or twisting your head)?
- Floor Space – Is there enough floor space in the trailer? You will probably never say that you would be happy to have less space so make sure it meets your needs. We travel with our two shepherds so we are always taking their needs into account. For example, can they each find a place to lay down and be out of the way? Is there enough space so they can both eat without being crowded; and we can still move around?

Keep in mind that a full slide-out could give you up to 18" more floor space than a partial slide-out.

- Layout – Does the overall flow of the floor plan make sense? Does the location of the bathroom make sense if you have visitors? When you enter the trailer you may want to come into the main living area; so if your entrance to the trailer is in the kitchen area will that cause any problems? We had a trailer where you entered into a narrow kitchen area. This design was very inconvenient. If someone came in while you were cooking you had to get out of the way; just so the person could pass by. Just keep these things in mind as you walk through the travel trailer.
- Heating and Air Conditioning – Look where your vents are located and make sure the layout of the vents make sense. As an example, if you have dogs you may want to make sure the floor vents are located in spots that don't present a paw hazard.

Kitchen
- Storage – Where the storage is located is as important as how much you have. You will

most likely be carrying dishes, pots and pans, and glasses. In order to cook or set your table they must be easily accessed. Make sure you are going to be able to easily reach items without reaching over tables, sofas, or people. Make sure that you are able to get to your kitchen storage and refrigerator with all of your slide-outs pulled in. When you are traveling down the road and want to quickly jump in the trailer to grab something you will be happy you didn't need to extend your slide room to make that possible.

- Pantry – I think a Pantry is necessary or at the very least a good number of well-located cabinets in which you can store all your dry and canned goods. If you feel you can get by with cabinets then make sure that all your dishes, pots and pans, and glassware still have a home somewhere. Our Coachmen Travel Trailer did not have a Pantry but it had a U-shaped kitchen. That kitchen had so many cabinets that we had more than enough room for food, pots and pans, dishes, appliances, and still had empty cabinets the we didn't even use.

- Counter Space – Oddly, most travel trailers today don't seem to have much counter space. Think about food prep areas and what you need

for appliances like a toaster, or coffee maker. It's a pain to pull out appliances and put them back after you use them because you have no useable counter space. You will never tell yourself that you should have LESS counter space.
- Outlets – Are the outlets available in areas that make sense? Is there an outlet located in a spot that makes sense for your toaster or coffee maker? We had a trailer that had the outlet located on the bottom of an overhead cabinet. This was the only one available for the coffee maker. Unfortunately the coffee makers cord wasn't long enough to reach the outlet.
- Trash Cabinet – Again, you don't see many trailers designed with these cabinets anymore. We have had these in the past and loved having them. Our last two Travel Trailers did not have a trash cabinet so we used a pedal trashcan that worked fine. If you don't have a trash cabinet, look at the layout of your kitchen and make sure you can find a spot to make a trash can work for you.
- Appliances – Make sure the refrigerator and freezer is large enough for the type of travel you are going to do. This does not mean that you should jump to thinking you need a

residential size. We have always been impressed with how much food we could pack in a standard RV refrigerator. Our family of four has had no problem lasting a week with this set-up. If you feel you absolutely must have a residential refrigerator, there are pro's and con's so make sure you understand what the power requirements are. Keep in mind that you may not be able to run a residential refrigerator on propane. If you like baking, then make sure your model has an oven, some do not. Make sure the microwave and cook top is big enough for the type and quantity of food you will prepare. Also make sure that the microwave is not mounted so high that you cannot easily access it.

Bathroom
- Toilet – Make sure that you can sit down comfortably without having your knees on the wall or door. Make sure that you can move easily around in the bathroom.
- Sink – You probably want to make sure that there is enough counter space that you have a place to set things down (like a curling iron or hair dryer for instance).

- Mirror – Make sure the mirror placement makes sense, and that it is big enough.
- Outlets – Are there enough electrical outlets and does their location make sense?
- Shower – Make sure you have room to shower without banging into the walls. Is the shower head high enough that you don't need to crouch down to wash your hair? Does the shower head turn off (without closing the hot and cold water taps) so you can save water while you shower? You may want to have shelves inside the shower to set body wash, shampoo, and conditioner. We have had showers with both shower curtains and glass doors…personally we are not going back to shower curtains.
- Storage – If you happen to have a closet in the bathroom, that's great! Having a closet allows you to actually shower and change in the bathroom versus dragging your clothes down to the bathroom with you. If you don't have a closet but you have ample cabinet space for towels and toiletries you may decide that is good enough. Not having enough space for towels, at a minimum, is a problem.

Outside the Trailer
- Power Tongue Jack – We have had both hand crank and power tongue jacks. With a power jack you won't be cranking up and down for ten minutes to get your hitch set up. I am guessing most rigs today are already equipped with power jacks, if not you may want to upgrade.
- Power/Manual Stabilizing Jacks – Stabilizing jacks can be manual crank down (by hand) or electric powered; we have had both. This is not a deal breaker issue for us. If we really liked a travel trailer model that didn't have power jacks we wouldn't hesitate to buy it. Manual jacks can be easily and quickly lowered with a portable drill and a socket that fits the jack nut.
- Storage – Make sure you have enough space to store everything you need to support the trailers systems. The travel trailer should have enough storage for your power cords, water hoses, sewer connections, tools, lawn chairs, grass mats, grill, jack stands if needed, portable dump station….you get the idea. Also make sure the access door to the storage area allows you to easily move bins or boxes in and out. A large storage area is great but if you can't easily move items in and out, that becomes a problem.

Having decent storage outside is just as important as inside.
- Outdoor Kitchen – We never felt this was a "must have" item, but now having had one on the last two trailers; we really enjoyed having it. Having an outdoor kitchen allows you to cook outside, keep cooking smells outside, and not heat up the inside of the trailer.
- Outdoor Shower – We have had travel trailers with and without an external shower. We prefer to have it for washing our kids' feet off, washing the dogs, and rinsing off our shoes if we happen to have a bad experience at the dog park.
- TV/Entertainment – Is having a TV outside important to you? If you enjoy watching football or other sports games this may be something you want to pay a little more for.
- RV Mounted Grill – Your travel trailer probably comes with this; if it doesn't you may want to find out how much that option costs. They are convenient because they plug into your existing propane line and are easy to store with a lot less mess than conventional grills. They typically mount on either the bumper or the side wall of the trailer. As a side note here, the Blackstone Griddle has become a popular

alternative to a grill for campers. An adapter can be purchased so you can connect it to your propane line just like a grill. Unlike the grill, the Blackstone is quite heavy.
- Ladder – We love having a ladder attached to the Travel Trailer. It makes getting on the RV so much easier. An alternative to this will not be safe or convenient. Keep in mind that you will be required to get on the roof for a number of reasons, the most important being roof inspections.
- Dump Valves – Understand where your grey and black water valves are located and how many there are. If the dump valve is located under a slide-out, that may be a problem.

In addition to just buying your RV, there are some very important steps that you will need to consider before you can tow it off the lot.

Tow Vehicle – Can your vehicle handle the weight of the trailer, more importantly can it handle the trailer fully loaded? You want a vehicle that can easily tow your load without struggling up hills. Please do not rely on the RV dealership to tell you what you can tow with your vehicle. It is your job to know the towing capacity of your vehicle. The dealership is only interested in selling you an RV.

Insurance – Don't forget to have your travel trailer included on your insurance policy. Nothing will ruin a trip faster than having a damaged trailer and no insurance. Also keep in mind that the insurance, depending on where you live, may not be inexpensive. It pays to research and shop for the best rates.

Storage – Determine where you will store your trailer when it is not being used. Don't assume that you can just park it in your driveway. Many home owners associations (aka Neighborhood Associations) will not allow this. Sometimes you may have a neighborhood where it is acceptable to park an RV and later the home owners association may change the rules (it has happened to us). Just make sure you factor in the monthly storage fees up front if necessary.

Hitch set up – Unless you tow a very, very light trailer (like a tear drop); you will need a weight distributing hitch. This is not just for your safety; it is for the safety of everyone on the road. Make sure you have your hitch set up professionally and that you understand how to set it up, and remove it, before you roll off the lot. Set up of the hitch should be second nature; if it isn't then you are flirting with danger. Read your owner's manual and make sure you follow all the appropriate maintenance as required. Please don't be the people at the campground that do not know how to unhook their new travel trailer so they start hitting the hitch with a hammer (sadly, this is a true story).

Electronic Brake Controller – This isn't a "nice to have", it's a necessity. This component applies the trailers brakes when you step on your tow vehicles brake pedal. Make sure you understand how to set your brake controller for travel. Always make sure it is in working condition before you leave on a trip.

Connectivity – If you have a job that allows you to travel or you just like to spend your time on the internet then think ahead for what you need in order to stay connected. Many campgrounds do not have Wi-Fi, or their Wi-Fi is substandard. So think about all your options for keeping connected on the road. In addition you may or may not have cable TV at the campground. When cable is available we have found that it is a much abbreviated version of what we have at home. If you need something more than what you can get at a campground, you have other options. There are portable satellite dishes and packages you can buy to make your entertainment experience on the road the same as you have at home.

In conclusion, no travel trailer is going to be perfect. They are like houses, once you move into them you realize certain things that might have been nicer to have, or things you would do differently in the future. The goal is to get something that you can feel comfortable living in for a few weeks at a time (or longer) without feeling like you have to modify the way you live.

Chapter 4 – Determining your Tow Vehicles Capabilities

If you want to have turmoil in your life you can ask one of three questions on-line.

1) What can my Vehicle Tow?
2) What Tires should I put on my Travel Trailer?
3) I'd like to buy travel trailer brand X but see a lot of problems on-line with it, is it a good trailer?

Anyone of those three questions ordinarily invokes the most base of responses from the on-line community. One only needs to visit a social media platform such as Facebook in order to see what kind of nastiness gets stirred up. Sadly, this is just the world we live in today; people are nice in person but quick to sarcasm on line.

I have come to the conclusion that these three subjects are like religion to people. They get so wrapped up in their personal preferences that they try to force their standard on anyone who might ask a question. There are many different tow vehicles, tires, and travel trailer brands. No person has experience with every brand of Travel Trailer, Tire or Tow Vehicle.

Tires and Travel Trailers are a personal preference decision based on the research that an individual undertakes. A tow vehicle, however, can only haul a specific weight limit safely. Therefore, prior to buying a Travel Trailer you either need to know what you can safely tow or you need to commit to buying a new vehicle that can tow your new travel trailer. There is really no other option unless you are going to rent or borrow a tow vehicle.

There are many towing guides that are published each year that will get you in the ball park of your tow vehicles capabilities but let's step through what you really need to know in order to tow within your limits.

- The Gross Vehicle Weight Rating (GVWR)

    This is the maximum allowable weight of the fully loaded tow vehicle plus your hitch. It is the maximum operating weight of your tow vehicle which includes the vehicle's frame, body, engine, engine fluids, fuel, accessories (like a bed topper for example), driver, passengers and cargo (excluding the trailer).

    You can find the Gross Vehicle Weight Rating on the sticker inside your driver's side door, however if you want to know what your vehicle weighs with all your camping cargo, then you need to load it as if you were going to go camping and then weigh it. Almost every truck stop has a scale, so locating one near you should be relatively easy.

Once you know the weight of your fully loaded truck for camping you can deduct that weight from the GVWR weight that you found on the door sticker. The remaining allowable weight is what is available for tongue weight.

- Tongue Weight

Knowing your remaining allowable weight is crucial to understanding how much weight you can tow and stay within your vehicle's limits. The Travel Trailer connects to your truck via the hitch and this transfer's weight onto the rear end of your truck. This additional weight also plays a role in how much you can tow. This number is referred to as "tongue weight". For travel trailers the target for tongue weight is somewhere between 10 to 15 percent of the weight of the travel trailer.

Keep in mind that when you look at the weight of a trailer at a dealership, this is the "Dry Weight" of the travel trailer. The dry weight is a completely empty travel trailer with nothing in the water or waste tanks. So when you load your camper with groceries, clothes, dishes, glassware, tools, hoses, grills, chairs, coolers, etc, the weight of the trailer goes up quite a bit. You should never exceed the GVWR of your travel trailer (which is found on the outside of your trailer). So for example my Dry weight is 7290 pounds, and my GVWR of the travel trailer (not truck) is 8950. This leaves me 1660 pounds for gear.

The tongue weight is the weight after you have loaded the travel trailer. If you use the dry weight of the trailer to calculate the tongue weight, your number will not be correct.

- Towing Capacity

This is what your truck manufacturer states as the towing capability of your truck. This number is affected by several factors such as the bed length, axle ratio, type of transmission (eg.6 speed), and engine size. Once you know the specifics of your vehicle you can find your vehicles towing capacity through the manufacturers towing guide which you can find on-line.

- Gross Combined Vehicle Weight Rating

This is the maximum allowable weight that your truck and travel trailer can weigh combined. So keep in mind that you could be within your payload and towing capacity but with your truck and trailer combined you could still exceed your Gross Combined Vehicle Weight Rating.

- EXAMPLE

Bob has a truck and looking at his manufacturers towing guide, it lists his truck as able to tow 10,500 pounds.

Bobs truck has a curb weight of 6900 lbs. and a gross vehicle weight rating of 8434 pounds. This leaves 1534 pounds. for cargo and passengers in the truck plus tongue weight. If Cargo, Passengers, and tongue weight exceed that number then towing with that truck is not a good decision.

In addition if the weight of the loaded trailer and the weight of the fully loaded vehicle exceed the Gross Combined Vehicle Weight Rating, towing with this truck is not a good idea.

So as an example let's pretend that Bobs travel trailer weighs 8000 lbs. and his fully loaded truck weighs 8400 pounds. That means his total weight is now 16400 pounds. Bob however, has a gross combined vehicle weight rating of 15000 pounds, so he has exceeded his GCVWR by 1400 lbs.

What is important to note in this example is that Bobs Truck Towing Guide states that he can tow 10500 pounds, so he is within the towing capacity but over the Gross Combined Vehicle Weight Rating.

Are you confused yet? You should be, because nothing is ever as clear as it seems when looking at the Manufacturers towing guide. This also tells you why you should never take a RV Dealerships word that your vehicle can tow your new travel trailer. There's no way they are going to go through all the mathematical gyrations it takes to make sure you are safe. They are there to sell you a Travel Trailer; it is your job to make sure you can tow it safely.

As a side note, I have run into the same confusion at truck dealerships when asking about towing capacity.

Chapter 5 – Selecting a Manufacturer

It probably goes without saying that this is an extremely important step in the purchase process. Not all manufacturers are created equal, even though the process they use to build trailers is basically the same.

Trailers are manufactured by hand; they are not constructed by robots (as in the auto industry). Perhaps someday this will be a reality, but until that happens we are purchasing units that may look the same but each one is somewhat unique. This is why two individuals may have the same model travel trailer and one may have no manufacturing issues while the other person does. Humans are fallible, and they construct your trailer.

So what does this mean? It is unrealistic to think that a new travel trailer will not have some issues. This is why we recommend using it often during the warranty period. You may hear folks on-line refer to a "Shake-Down Trip". They are talking about discovering (shaking out) all the issues with a new trailer.

Every Manufacturer is going to have travel trailers that come off the line with issues. They may try to catch them all before they get to the dealership but many issues slip through the cracks and end up being fixed during the warranty period.

One of the most important things to consider when purchasing a travel trailer is the company that manufactured it. Almost everything you need to know can be found on line. Here are some of the questions you need to answer regarding the manufacturer (we will touch on the dealerships later).

How is their travel trailer constructed? Not all trailers are manufactured using the same materials and construction techniques. Even the frames of the trailers can be different; Wood or Aluminum. Then there are the sidewalls. For instance, one manufacturer of Travel Trailers manufactures walls made of a product called Azdel. The Manufacturer claims this material is impervious to water therefore you will not need to worry about exterior delamination if you should get a water leak. Other manufacturers are using Fiberglass laminated onto wood and foam, while others may use aluminum siding. All of these different constructions have pros and cons. Do your research and determine what is most important to you.

What is the manufacturer's track record on repairs? Do they have a large number of recalls? Are there a large number of unhappy customers who swear they would never buy another travel trailer from them? Can you find instances where they just refuse to stand behind their products? Most of this information you can find through blogs on the internet. However, remember that unhappy customers tend to post more than happy ones that are busy camping.

How is the Manufacturers Customer Service structured? Can you call the manufacturer and get through to an agent to help you with a problem during the warranty period? Will they send a mobile repair company to your campsite if you have something that goes wrong? In a perfect world the trailers would never have anything fail, but this is the real world. A great customer support team can alleviate a lot of strife between the customer and the manufacturer.

Here's a quick personal example to illustrate my point. On one travel trailer that we owned the rear electric jack pads failed in the down position (while under warranty). The manufacture required that I find some way to make it to the local dealership for repairs. I spent an hour on my back under the trailer disassembling and bungee cording the cross members together in order to get to my dealership. On our next trailer (different manufacturer), we had a water leak where a screw had rubbed on a water line under the sink. Thankfully we were in the trailer when we heard the leak start. The manufacturer immediately authorized a mobile RV repair tech to come to our campsite and fix the issue. This quick repair saved our camping trip. So what you see here are two different manufacturers with two different approaches for servicing their customer.

    Also please keep in mind that the specific travel trailer brand name doesn't necessarily give an indication of the parent company that owns that manufacturer. Many companies went out of business back in 2008, and were gobbled up by conglomerates. So now, although you may be purchasing a well-known brand, it is not the same company it once was. Now for example it may be under the umbrella of Thor Industries, Berkshire Hathaway, or one of the other large conglomerates. Why is this important? It's important because you may want to look at how happy the customers are across that entire Company as policies (customer service etc.) are set at the top and trickle down.

Chapter 6 - Selecting a Dealership

Now that you have decided on a manufacture it's time to investigate which dealership to purchase from.

Remember the old slogan "The Sales Department sells the first vehicle but the Service Department sells the second"? Never was this more accurate than in the world of recreational vehicles. Of the seven RV dealerships that we have done business with, I could in good conscience only recommend perhaps two.

Since I almost always did well on my financial dealings on the purchase, this really comes down to service. Let's face it; the sales team at the dealership wants to do whatever it can to seal the deal. However, when you pull that unit off their lot what is your experience going to be when you need to get it repaired or serviced?

Almost always the Sales Team is going to tell you that getting your unit serviced will be no issue. Almost always this is untrue. Investigate the dealerships service record on quality and how long it takes to get things repaired. Having a great deal on a camper is going to be very unsatisfying if you find something wrong and it sits on the dealerships lot for most of the camping season, while you are making your payments.

It would be nice to say that I am exaggerating, but I am not. The internet is full of stories from new RV buyers that sat out the camping season while their new travel trailer sat for months waiting for repairs to be completed at their dealership. Guess what else was happening? That's right; their warranty period was evaporating at the same time. Many times the buyers ended up calling and complaining to the manufacturer only to find out that the dealers service department had been untruthful about why the delay was taking place.

Another frustrating situation is getting your trailer back from the dealer and discovering it had not been fixed correctly. It's a well-known fact that the industry is lacking qualified service personnel. This is why there is a growing industry of independent repair facilities. It has been our experience that what takes months for an RV dealership to take care of can be accomplished in a day or two at one of these facilities. So make sure you find out if that is an avenue that is open to you during the warranty period, but inquire this of the manufacturer not the dealership. You need to get it from the horse's mouth.

One of my trailers was returned to me after warranty work where they replaced the kitchen sink. The sink was replaced because their technician scratched it taking off the manufacturer's sticker. This technician had used a razor blade on a plastic sink. That should have been a sign to the service department that they had a personnel problem, or a training problem, or both. When I turned on the water I found that he had not remembered to hook up the water lines to the sink. Imagine how disappointed and angry I was as water began to fill up the cabinets on a brand new travel trailer. Not only was this a major mistake but where is the oversite in the dealerships service department?

That's not to say that all dealerships have horrible service departments but my personal opinion is that this is a growing problem. Seek out others that have purchased from this dealership and find out what their real life experiences are. If you find that a repetitive theme of bad experience exists, then find a different dealership. It is better to drive three hours to find a decent dealer than be at the mercy of a bad dealership five minutes away.

A word of caution as it applies to warranty work. The State you purchase your travel trailer in may require that while you are under warranty it must be serviced by the Selling Dealership. We found this to be the case in the state we currently live, there could be others. So in this case, finding the dealership with the best service is key.

You can also search online blogs for reviews of dealerships as well as the Better Business Bureau or state consumer protection agency to get an indication of how they conduct business. A couple of hours of research may save you hours of time down the road.

Chapter 7 – What The Dealership Won't Tell You

1. That your vehicle can not tow the trailer you're interested in purchasing.

 To be quite honest, this really isn't their job. More than likely the salesperson is going to tell you that anything you bring to the lot "is just fine". Please do not rely on a travel trailer salesperson to decide what you can safely tow. It is your responsibility to know what your tow capacities are and to have the correct hitch for your tow vehicle and trailer.

2. The Travel Trailer does not come ready to go.

 There are essential supplies that you are going to need in order to go camping. Things that will not come with your new travel trailer will be the sewer hose, fresh and black water hoses, black and grey tank chemicals, jack pads, and perhaps a battery. We will touch on more about the essentials later on in the book. Be prepared, these are startup costs that you need to budget for.

3. Not everything is covered during the warranty period

These are not automobiles with bumper to bumper coverage during the warranty. You need to maintain certain parts of your RV during the warranty period or your warranty will be void. Make sure you <u>understand everything</u> that you are responsible for maintaining so you don't get an ugly surprise at some point. Almost all of this information is contained in your owner's manual.

As an example, you are responsible for inspecting your travel trailers roof and sealing any voids during the warranty. You may want to pay your dealership to do this versus climbing on top of the trailer, but it needs to be done to keep your warranty in place. Don't get lulled into thinking that just because your roof membrane has a 10 year warranty that you don't need to do anything – you most certainly do.

4. That you should get an independent inspection.

There is no way that the Dealership is going to recommend this, because it might just ruin their sale. The Dealer Pre-Sale inspections are horribly superficial. Please see the next chapter (chapter 8), on why this is perhaps the most important thing you need to do PRIOR to signing any paperwork at the Dealership.

5. That there is no Lemon Law for Travel Trailers

There really isn't a lemon law for travel trailers, perhaps with the exception of California. In fact the RV industry has fought to make sure there are no lemon laws for recreational vehicles. While the balance of the states may have some limited protection; this limited protection ordinarily comes from what is sometimes referred to as the Federal RV Lemon Law. The Federal RV Lemon Law is actually the Magnuson-Moss Act.

So what is the Magnuson-Moss Act? The Magnuson-Moss act was enacted by Congress in response to the widespread misuse of express warranties and disclaimers. The purpose of the act is to make warranties on consumer products more easily understood and enforceable. It protects RV owners when the manufacturer fails to honor their written warranty. This law applies to motorized RV's (Class A, Class B and Class C motorhomes) as well as Travel

Trailers, Toy Haulers, Fifth-Wheel Trailers and Truck Campers.

If there is a problem, the manufacturer must repair the vehicle in a reasonable amount of time and within a reasonable number of attempts. You should keep meticulous records of all your phone calls, emails, and texts to the dealer and manufacturer. Also keep a record of the amount of time the RV was unusable due to the problem(s).

Lastly if the manufacturer has failed to repair the RV after a reasonable time and opportunity; this is the point where you will probably want to seek legal advice from a recreational vehicle lemon law attorney.

Since there really isn't a good lemon law for most RV Owners, there are a number of things you, as a buyer should do:

Research the RV you are thinking of purchasing. Look at RV Lemon Law websites at the brand and model that you are interested in and if it has a large number of complaints. Research the company you want to buy from. Go on social media and see what the common problems are with your potential RV. Look for red flags around the quality and the manufacturers willingness to make things right.

As we mentioned above, have an independent RV inspection done prior to purchasing a new RV. If the RV Dealership tells you that they won't allow an independent inspection before you sign a purchase agreement; run away from that dealer. A trustworthy dealership will not mind if you have an independent inspection.

There was a time when most attorneys were not interested in RV Warranty litigation. That seems to be changing now as many are actually advertising this service. Always consider your alternatives before living with a problem that should have been fixed.

6. The Sales contract is written to protect the dealership

This probably goes without saying, given the discussions above, but have a thorough understanding of what your rites are as a consumer and what recourse you have before you sign on the dotted line. Look for clauses in the contract that may put you at risk, you may be signing certain rights away. Also keep in mind that legal recourse may take place where the trailer is manufactured, not where you may have purchased it.

7. Not everything on the trailer is top of the line.

Most manufacturers are buying in bulk and obviously trying to maximize their profits. Tires are almost always a good example of this. We have almost always had to replace the tires that the manufacturer placed on the vehicle. I'm not saying that this will always be the case but just be aware of all the details on the travel trailer that you are purchasing.

Chapter 8 - Getting an Independent Inspection

Having an independent Travel Trailer Inspection, is it necessary? The Short answer is yes…the Long answer is yes!

I'm going to start by saying that Tammy and I have been buying travel trailers for just about 30 years. The quality and or quality control has steadily been going downhill since then.

A case in point, our first travel trailer was a 1971 JayWren by Jayco. We purchased the JayWren in 1989 for I believe around 900 dollars. This trailer had already seen better days as it was 18 years old. Despite the weathered exterior and the worn cushions on the interior, this trailer was solid. It was built strong to stand up to whatever Mother Nature could dish out. For a sixteen foot trailer though, it was heavy, and that was due to the heavy-duty construction. Even after 18 years of service, everything worked on this trailer; furnace, refrigerator, wiring, and plumbing, absolutely everything worked. It was a testament to the folks at Jayco that built it.

Does anyone buying a travel trailer today feel that their new travel trailer will be solid in 18 years? Probably not, and why is that?

It is a result of the manufacturers' emphasis on pushing even more new trailers out the door, the employee incentives to drive the production higher, and the manufacturers' poor quality control.

It's obvious that the golden age of quality built travel trailers is pretty much over. Add to this fact that the Pre-delivery Inspections (PDI's) really are a joke, regardless of whether they are happening at the manufacturer or the dealer facility.

We currently have a 2017 Grand Design travel trailer, and we love it, but it hasn't been without some major issues. These are issues that should have easily been caught in their three separate Pre-Delivery Inspections (PDI). A manufacturer telling you that they have three separate PDIs on each trailer sounds great on paper but unfortunately too many issues still end up with the buyer (that's you). So please consider the PDI to be nothing more than the sellers' talking point.

I am only using Grand Design as an example in this case as all manufacturers have a PDI.

That being said, Grand Design, in my opinion, currently has the best customer service on

the planet while you are under warranty.
However, let's be realistic, no one wants to buy a rig and then spend months fixing what should have come out of the factory correct. I understand that these trailers bounce down the road, and that they are handmade, but so was the 1971 Jayco.

The long and the short of it, is that these trailers could be made better if the manufacturer wanted it that way. Sadly there is no incentive for the manufacturer to make that happen as consumers are buying more travel trailers now than ever before.

Technology has changed over the years with the addition of complicated electronics, slide rooms, more intricate plumbing and lighting. Obviously there is a lot more that can go wrong today than could ever fail on a 1971 Jayco. That means there are more components that should be inspected at the manufacturer and dealer and more things to miss during that inspection.

Given the above issues, we believe that every new buyer (and even those that are buying a used travel trailer) should invest the money to have an independent travel trailer inspection done. Before you sign any papers at the dealership tell them you are going to have an independent inspection done. If the dealer states that they won't allow that without a purchase agreement first, then run away.

Trust me, the gold standard today at most dealerships when it comes to their own inspections, are superficial at best…if they happen at all. They just go through the travel trailer and look for the obvious and glaring issues. They are not going to conduct a thorough inspection like a certified RV inspector is going to do.

So how do you find an inspector and what is the cost? The NRVIA is the best place to find an inspector to look at your impending purchase.

The National Recreational Vehicle Inspectors Association (NRVIA) is an organization providing certifications for professional recreational vehicle inspectors across North America. NRVIA Inspectors are required to follow specific standards. These standards will ensure that you will receive a professional, standardized, and thorough travel trailer inspection.

You will want to find a "Level 2" inspector, and you should expect to pay about $400.00 for the service. This is a very in-depth inspection covering 44 major inspection points. Under each major inspection point there are multiple check points. Here is an example of one travel trailer inspection check point:

Checkpoint #4 – Exterior Components

4.0 – Roof

4.1 – Roof Type

4.2 – General condition of the roof

4.3 – Joints and Seals

4.4 – Vents

4.5 – Vent covers

4.6 – Plumbing vents

4.7 – Air Conditioning Covers and Exterior Coils

4.8 – Ladder

4.9 – Satellite Antenna

4.10 – Radio Antenna

4.11 – Refrigerator Vent

4.12 – Skylight(s)

4.13 – Storage Containers

4.14 – Spot lights

4.15 – Air Horns (N/A for Travel Trailers)

4.16 – Solar Panels

4.17 – Signs of Equipment removed

Now do you think that anyone at the RV dealership is going to take the time to do this type of inspection (and keep in mind that this example is only 1 of the 44 check points)? I can tell you with a great deal of certainty (based on our last four purchases) that it is not happening. The emphasis is on selling – not inspecting (or in my humble opinion - service).

Most RVIA inspectors will let you know if they find a major problem while they are inspecting the unit so that you can decide at that point if you even want them to proceed with the rest of the inspection.

I realize $400.00 is a lot of money, but problems that may surface after your travel trailer warranty is up are costly as well. Problems that occur during the warranty period may be covered from a cost perspective, but may ruin your camping season. The internet is replete with stories from owners of brand new travel trailers that missed the entire camping season; while their trailer was hostage in a dealer's service department.

It would seem that given the environment today it would be wise for everyone to get a pre-purchase inspection from someone who has no ties to the Manufacturer or Dealership.

Our Advice is to get the independent inspection <u>even if you decide to buy a used travel trailer.</u> You can locate an inspector at www.nrvia.org

Chapter 9 - What Is A Walk-Through?

Just like a stick and brick house, you will have an opportunity to inspect your travel trailer prior to signing any paperwork at the dealership. If they try to get you to sign paperwork before this, then leave the dealership. Any dealership that wants you to sign before an inspection is shady. There are plenty of honest RV Dealerships, so stay away from the ones with poor business practices.

As mentioned in the previous chapter you really should consider an independent inspection of your travel trailer prior to purchase. The inspector will be more thorough and have test equipment that is not available to you as a buyer. Having an independent inspection does not mean that you shouldn't walk through the unit as well and check everything you possibly can. An extra set of eyes never hurt anyone.

While the following list may not be all-inclusive (because every travel trailer is different), it will certainly get you in the ball park of what you need to be inspecting. You may wish to copy this list and take it with you to the dealership. Don't let the salesperson rush you through your walk-through. This is a huge investment you are making – it needs to be done on your terms.

Interior of the Travel Trailer

- Look at the ceiling and walls. Can you see any signs of water damage?
- Do the cabinet doors open and close correctly, and do they stay closed when shut? Do drawers slide in and out easily and stay closed when shut? Do they all looked aligned properly and is the finish flawless?
- Do all the shelves in the cabinets appear to be solid?
- Check all closets and make sure that any hanger bars or shelving is secure. Make sure the doors open and close properly and are secure when closed.
- Does the furniture operate correctly? For example, the recliners operate easily and the sofa sleepers fold out correctly. If you have a bunk bed set-up, make sure those beds are properly secured.
- Check that you can access the storage under the bed easily. Make sure that it is not hard to lift and stays in the upright position for loading/unloading.

- Look at ceiling trim and wall trim throughout the trailer. Make sure that you identify any loose, broken, or cracked pieces of trim. Remember trim is more than just wood trim, there is also wall trim between wall panels.
- Inspect your flooring and make sure it is installed correctly. This includes all vinyl and carpeting. Also make sure that there is no damage from slide rooms opening and closing.
- Test all of your appliances, stove, refrigerator, oven, microwave, and television etc. Make sure all operate correctly.
- Run your air conditioner and furnace. Make sure both perform as expected.
- All fabrics and solid surfaces should be free of tears, dents, and scratches. This includes your table top and counter top material.
- Inspect all the sinks for scratches and dents.
- Find your power control panel and make sure all switches work and you understand what every switch operates. Typically these panels will include lights, slide rooms, and tank sensor displays.
- Make sure all Fire, Propane, and CO2 detectors are in working order.

- Make sure every light and every light switch works correctly.
- Make sure you can test, and reset any GFI outlet.
- Test any USB ports, all new trailers come with these.
- Make sure all electrical outlets are working; you may want to use a three wire receptacle tester which you can find at any hardware store for around five dollars. The tester will identify any issues with the way the outlet is wired.
- Test every vent fan for correct operation, and that every vent opens and closes easily
- Every slide-out should function smoothly, and the seals should have no gaps so that water and/or pests are prevented from entering the trailer.
- Make sure you can unlock and open the windows easily. Also make sure when you close them that they lock securely in place. You would be surprised how many times there is an issue with a window not locking.
- Make sure that any curtains or mini blinds work.
- Run water in every sink and shower. Make sure that there are no leaks in the water lines

going to the faucets and no links coming from the P-Traps under each drain.
- Inspect the shower enclosure for any issues, and make sure it has no soft spots in the floor underneath the shower pan.
- Inspect and towel bars or hooks throughout the trailer and make sure they are connected securely to the wall.

Exterior of the Travel Trailer

- How does the exterior look, is the fiberglass or aluminum siding without seams and dents? Look for any delamination in fiberglass walls.
- Look at the seals around the windows, cargo doors, and slide-outs. Make sure they are not cracked, shrunk, or cut too short so that they are not covering the complete exterior frames.
- Inspect the tires for dry rot, cracking, nails, and gouges.
- Check the frame if possible and make sure all the welding looks complete.
- Inspect the undercarriage and make sure the springs/suspension looks rust free and undamaged. Also look for any loose wires or wires that appear to be unprotected.

- If the underside of the trailer is insulated make sure that it is intact with no open holes or tears, and that it is not sagging.
- Check the wiring harness in front of the trailer. Make sure that the casing is intact and that there are no frayed or broken wires.
- Make sure the battery is present and that the connections are clean.
- Inspect any exterior accessories and make sure that they operate accordingly. This includes any outside entertainment center, outdoor kitchen, cargo doors, ladders, and spare tire carrier.
- Make sure any cargo door or entrance door locks and unlocks easily and has good seals.
- Make sure the entrance door deadbolt locks completely and easily.
- Make sure that the Screen door easily latches to the exterior door.
- Inspect your roof and make sure that no voids exist in the sealant and that all openings for AC, vents, skylights, etc, are sealed completely. Make sure no rips, holes or tears exist in the roofing membrane.
- Check the operation of the awning. Regardless of if it is manual or electric you will want to

make sure that it operates freely and that the fabric is flawless.
- Make sure any exterior lights are functional; this includes the front CAP lights if so equipped.
- Make sure any outlets are functional. REMEMBER – more than likely there will be lights and outlets on the inside of your cargo area.
- Make sure that the T-Handle dump valves for black and gray water tanks operate freely. Keep in mind, there may be more than one set on your Travel Trailer.
- Fold and unfold the entry steps. They should open and close without binding. There should not be a significant amount of flex present when you use them.
- Open and close the Hand Rail for the entry steps. It should open and close easily.
- Test hooking up the power supply cord to the travel trailer. It should plug and or fasten to the trailer without a lot of difficulty. Keep in mind 50 amp cords are going to be a little harder to finesse.

Chapter 10 – When To Sign On The Dotted Line

So at this point in your journey (after the inspections etc.) you are going to be thinking one of three things.

1. This is definitely the Travel Trailer for us!
2. This Trailer has some issues but I think it will work out!
3. This trailer has a lot of issues that I don't want to deal with!

I would recommend that if you are thinking anything other than number 1 above, you should look for another Travel Trailer. Never settle for something that may "work out". There are hundreds of different travel trailer models and manufacturers. It makes no sense to put up with a trailer that is either poor quality or barely meets your needs.

Trust me when I say that if you settle, you will either be looking for another travel trailer sooner than you think, or you will decide that camping this way is not for you.

Most importantly, discuss all your reservations about the travel trailer with your significant other if you are not a lone buyer. You both may be thinking something negative about the trailer but not mention it, and then later you may wish that you had. The time to flush out any worries about your purchase is now.

If you fall into the category "This is definitely the Travel Trailer for us", then it is time to sign the paperwork.

Chapter 11 – Knowing What Steps I Need To Perform

Now you may be wondering how this chapter relates to buying a travel trailer. Well the Dealership is probably not going to do a very good job educating you on how your Travel Trailer works. Therefore you will want to know as much as you can before you leave the dealership with your new travel trailer. If you don't understand what is expected of you as an owner the first time you go to a campground you may feel unprepared and confused.

Don't forget your best friend will be your owner's manual; however it may be somewhat generic. So what are the things you will want to know before you leave the dealership so you can set up correctly at camp? Here's a brief list you should go through with your dealer:

Where is the power cord and how do I connect it? Is it a 30 amp system or a 50 amp system? It's important to know the difference as the campsites will need to have the service specific to your trailer.

Where are the fuses located? Don't wait until you're under the gun at 2:00AM in the morning trying to locate fuses.

Where is the hook up for the water hose? Some are inside the storage area; some are on the exterior of the RV.

How do I switch between city water and just running off the fresh water tank?

Where is the water pump switch?

Where is the hot water heater located? This is important so that you can bypass the water heater during winterization of the travel trailer. You also need to know how to access the water heater drain plug on the outside of the travel trailer. This is so you can drain your water heater after each use.

How does the hot water heater operate? There is probably an electric and propane option. Understand how to operate in either mode.

How do the slide rooms operate? There are three different types of slide mechanisms; you need to know the operating procedures for your model.

How do the furnace and any air conditioners operate and how does the thermostat work?

How do I flush out the black tank?

Where are ALL the dump handles (Grey and Black)? Keep in mind you may have more than one handle for each type of tank. I once had a travel trailer that had two grey dump valves, one for the kitchen and one for the bath.

How do I attach my sewer hose? This is important as a mistake can be embarrassing for you and entertaining for your neighbors. Also, you may have more than one sewer connection. Our 2007 Coachmen had two sewer connections, and that made dumping the tanks complicated. It's hard with a set up like that to always get perfectly centered with the sewer at a campground.

How does the front jack work? There are manual and electric models.

How do the leveling jacks operate? Some are manual and some are electric.

How do all my appliances operate? Keep in mind your refrigerator usually can run on either electric or propane. Understand how to switch between the two different settings.

How does the TV work? Most have a booster if you are using TV with the roof antenna. If you have a roof antenna that extends, make sure you understand how to extend it and retract it. If you want to use a satellite dish find out how the cable coming into the unit needs to be connected. It is typically connected differently for antenna vs. satellite. If you are using satellite TV you will not want to be using your booster.

How do I secure the inside of the travel trailer for traveling? Certain doors and showers may need to be fastened using straps or bands etc. Make sure you understand what is required before you go down the road and have a loose door put a hole in your interior wall.

How do I secure the outside of the travel trailer for travel? Know how to fold your entry steps and understand how to lock all your storage and entrance doors.

Chapter 12 – What Are The Essentials For Getting On The Road

When you buy a new Travel Trailer, you can be sure of one thing; what you see is what you get! When you buy that RV on the lot it is not going to come with a hitch for your vehicle, a fresh water hose, a hose for the black tank wash out, a sewer hose, wheel chocks, blocks for under your jack, coax for the cable television hookup, or a power cord extension. All of those items you will need to purchase before you go camping, and that's just to get you on the road to the campground. In addition you will still need to buy additional items for inside the travel trailer (silverware, plates, pans, etc.). So as you can see, you've only just begun to spend money with the purchase of your travel trailer.

Now that doesn't mean you need to start filling your trailer with every imaginable furnishing like it is a house. In fact if you approach the RV kitchen as if it has to include every gadget you have at home, you will quickly be pushing the limit of your carrying capacity. Am I joking? Not really! Kitchen accessories can weigh a lot. Also place heavier objects lower in cabinets so they don't fall over and out of an overhead cabinet, damaging a floor or countertop.

This fact also applies to things like cases of soda, or large containers full of dog food. The heavier the item, the closer to the floor it should be.

Be conservative in your approach. You probably don't need a bread maker, an electric can opener, a waffle maker, a 12 piece dinner service etc. Remember what goes in has to eventually come out too. Take what makes your camping experience easy and convenient without jamming the travel trailer from wall to wall.

Keep in mind everything you bring adds to the weight of the trailer. Make sure you have the basics covered first and then proceed in a reasonable fashion.

Chapter 13 - Creating A Warranty Punch List

This will be one of the most important things you will need to do after the Purchase. Remember, it is unrealistic to think that you will not find something wrong with your travel trailer during the warranty period. These trailers are made by hand so there will be issues that need to be addressed even if they are minor.

Create a punch list like the one below (a work of fiction in this case) that captures all information:

Issue	Screen Door won't latch
Date Identified	10/20/2019
Date Dealer Notified	10/21/2019
Dealership	Texans RV HQ
Dealers Phone Number	555-555-5555
Dealer Representative	John Doe
Scheduled Appt Time	11/1/2019
Fixed? (yes or No)	No
Notes:	Dealer states it cannot be repaired

Manufacturer Notified	Grand Design
Date MFG Notified	11/2/2019
Manufacturers Phone Number	
Manufacturer's Representative	Joe Jones
Notes:	Is following up with the Dealership MFG will contact me in 24 hours.

Obviously the more information you can document the better off you will be should a dispute occur around warranty work (or in a worst case scenario you need to contact an attorney).

Remember it is your job to document and report everything in a timely manner. I have had punch lists that had over 25 items on them. Keep a record of everything no matter how large or how small you think the issue is.

Also, don't be afraid to follow up early and often with your dealership on repairs. The squeaky wheel gets the grease. If you are content to let your trailer sit on their lot, chances are they will be too. Tell the dealership when you drop off your travel trailer what your expectations are for timely repair. If at any point during the repair process you are dissatisfied with what is happening then reach out to your manufacturer for help, and document every conversation. I believe that in most cases the Manufacturer wants to know where bad service is taking place.

Chapter 14 - Beyond The Basics, What Is Needed

There is a good reason for travel trailer mods (modifications) or accessories. They make camping safer, and more enjoyable with less worry.

When you buy a new Travel Trailer, you will be required to purchase some basic items to get started! As we mentioned above, when you buy that RV on the lot it is not going to come with a hitch for your vehicle, a fresh water hose, a hose for the black tank wash out, a sewer hose, wheel chocks, blocks for under your jack, or a power cord extension. All of those items you will need to get before you go camping, and that's just to get you on the road to the campground.

In addition, you will still need to buy items for inside the travel trailer just to live day to day while you are on the road (silverware, plates, pans, etc.).

Beyond those fundamentals what are the most important products you will want to add to your trailer to enjoy trouble-free camping? Here are what we feel are the eight most important things (Accessories or Travel Trailer Mods) you will want to purchase:

A surge protector. These are not cheap but they are a lot less expensive than replacing the electrical components in your travel trailer. These can be hard-wired inside your travel trailer or you can get a portable unit that you plug into the power pedestal at the campground. We have the portable 50 Amp Model, EMS-PT50X by Progressive Industries. This unit looks at a number of conditions like, over/under voltage, reverse polarity, power surges, and power pedestals not wired correctly. Then if it detects a problem it immediately shuts the power down coming into your trailer. It will also display an error code in the event of a problem so you can resolve it. Remember, it only takes one lightning strike nearby to ruin a camping trip. The EMS (Electrical Management System) is well worth the money.

An adjustable Water Pressure Regulator. These are really very inexpensive; around $30.00 dollars so there is no reason to not have one. You can spend less on a non-adjustable model that always holds your water at 40 PSI. Water pressure at campgrounds is unpredictable so having a way to restrict high pressure is necessary. Most RV plumbing lines cannot handle pressure above 50

PSI, and it may be even lower on older trailers. I adjust my pressure regulator to about 45 PSI, just to be safe. Don't risk having a ruptured line in your trailer.

A Tire Pressure Monitoring System. You only need to look on-line to see all the damage created to a travel trailer by a blowout. Most travel trailer owners are not even aware that they have a flat tire until they have driven a long distance. This results in hundreds of dollars' worth of damage to their rim, exterior, and under carriage of their trailer. There are many units on the market so do your research. We use the Tire Minder TPMS, and have been very happy with it. It tells us the tire pressure and tire temperature. Temperature can be just as damaging, as it will cause a blow out as well and may be a sign of a deeper issue such as rubbing brake shoes or a bad wheel bearing.

Bug Screens for your furnace, refrigerator, and water heater. Don't let mud daubers, wasps, or other critters damage your expensive equipment. These are easy to attach and prevent a lot of damage. Since they attach with springs or zip ties, they are easy to remove if you choose to run your equipment with them off and only have them on during storage. We have used them for years and never taken them off but we know others that remove them when camping.

Decent Trailer Tires. In my opinion not many travel trailer manufacturers use decent tires; Jayco may be the exception as they have recently moved to putting Goodyear Endurance tires on their units. Read the reviews on-line of the tires you have on your trailer and make sure they are decent tires. We have put new tires on the last four trailers we purchased within the first year. While we have moved to the Endurance tires, there are a few good brands out there so you do have options…do your research.

A Water Filter. You might be surprised what water you may get at a campground. We filter ours, and you may want to as well. We bought a filter that connects to the faucet at the campground, we then put our hose on the filter and we are good to go. There are many options for water filters and many options for where you can add them to your trailer.

An Observation/Back up Camera. We went with an observation camera as it can be used when we drive so we know what is happening behind us before we change lanes. It also doubles as a backup camera...but I rely more on Tammy for backing up as the camera doesn't help me with any blind side when I am turning the camper on an angle. The real advantage for us has been using it on the road.

A Camco Screen Door Grille. This is a necessity if you travel with dogs or small children. It prevents them from pushing through the screen on your travel trailer door. It takes about ten minutes to install, and looks nice.

So that concludes our list of what we feel are the eight most important travel trailer mods/accessories to add to your comfort and safety.

Chapter 15 – Creating A Check List

How many times have you traveled 25 miles down the road only to realize you forgot something at home? If this has happened to you then you may be a good candidate for creating a list so you can check off the essentials before you leave home with a travel trailer. The list below assumes that you are departing from your home base and that the travel trailer's black and grey tanks are empty.

Let's start with some of the basics; these can be done prior to the day of departure.

- Confirm your reservations at your campground. We print our confirmations and take them with us.
- Stop your mail with the post office.
- Let someone know your travel plans so they can alert you of any suspicious activity.
- Make sure you have addresses for all your campground stops. We load our destinations into Garmin in advance of the trip.
- Make sure you have your RV registration and insurance in your tow vehicle, you never know when you will need it.

- A day or two before you leave it is not a bad idea to start your refrigerator so it's at an appropriate temperature when you load your groceries.
- Make sure your RV Battery is fully charged.
- Make sure your Propane Tanks are full.
- If you are taking city water, then fill your RV water tank.
- Pack emergency supplies, this would include a first aid kit, flashlights, etc…
- Pack a basic tool kit and a tire pressure gauge.
- Inspect the entire hitch assembly, tighten all bolts to the manufacturers' specification, and grease the assembly if necessary.
- Check the tire pressure on the Travel Trailer.
- Check the tire pressure on the tow vehicle.
- Gas up the tow vehicle and add any needed fluids (like windshield washer fluid).

A day before the trip

- Pack up all your clothes, shoes, jackets, rain gear, boots, and hats, needed for the trip.
- Pack bedding and pillows.
- Bath towels and Pool towels.

- Load all of your groceries into the trailer.
- If your refrigerator has been running on electric, then you need to decide if you will run on propane as you travel or shut all your propane off the day you leave and hope the refrigerator stays cold enough until you park your camper. There are many opinions about traveling with or without propane on…obviously the safest method is to run without propane on. If you turn it off, do so at the tanks as well.
- Install bracing bars in the refrigerator and pantry if needed to prevent shifting of food and supplies during travel.
- Double check that water heater drain plug is installed and that the water heater has been taken off by-pass if this is you first trip of the season.
- Kitchen supplies, dishes, pots, pans, glasses, silverware, napkins.
- Load any entertainment items such as games, or movies.
- Load any outdoor equipment needed (grill, chairs, lawn mats, etc).

- Make sure you have toilet chemicals, RV toilet paper, and any cleaning supplies (this would include hand soap, dish soap, paper towels).
- If you travel with pets make sure you have a copy of their vaccination records.
- Pet Food and pet supplies (toys, kennel, bowls, spare leashes, tie outs, poo bags, etc…)
- Make sure you have all your sewer, fresh water, and black water hoses and supplies.

The day you leave

- Toiletries like toothbrushes, toothpaste, shampoo, body wash, etc…
- Prescriptions.
- Pet medications.
- Lock TV into place.
- Close roof vents and any open windows.
- Lower antenna if it is up.
- Turn off Furnace/AC.
- Secure any pocket or shower doors, and close any internal doors.
- Tie Down freestanding chairs if necessary.
- Secure refrigerator and oven doors if they are supplied with latching mechanisms.

- Retract Awning.
- Retract slide rooms.
- Disconnect land line power supply and stow power cord.
- Raise stabilizer jacks and stow any leveling pads.
- Hitch Tow Vehicle to Travel Trailer.
- Plug RV into tow vehicle.
- Remove wheel chocks.
- Walk around vehicle and make sure all storage doors and RV doors are locked.
- put steps up and fold back door railing if you have one.
- Make sure all valve covers are on (sewer cap, fresh water cap, etc...).
- Double check hitch assembly and emergency brake-away cable.
- Check brake lights and turn signals on RV.
- Check trailer brake operation and adjust if necessary.

As you leave

- Spare set of house keys, travel trailer, and tow vehicle keys. Remember if you get somehow locked out of your travel trailer you need a backup plan. Hannah once locked Tammy out of the RV by putting her paw on the dead-bolt lever. When I came back from getting my oil changed, Tammy was waiting at the picnic table while both dogs were locked up in the RV. Who would have thought? Now we carry multiple sets of keys so no matter what crazy scenario takes place we are covered.

- All appliances in your personal dwelling are turned off.
- House is locked up.
- Security cameras and alarms activated.
- Garage door is down.
- All gates are locked.

This may not be an all-inclusive list but hopefully it provides a blue print for a list that you can construct that will get rid of that "I know I forgot something" feeling.

Chapter 16 - What Is A Shakedown Trip?

A shakedown trip is a common expression that you will hear new travel trailer owners use. The Shakedown trip is really just an initial camping trip where the owner uses the new RV and tries to "Shake Out" any potential problems.

This is not to say that one trip is going to shake out all the potential issues that a new or even used travel trailer may have. The best thing an owner can do during the manufacturer's warranty period is to use the camper as much as possible. It may take several trips before all of issues are identified.

In our case with our newest travel trailer, we were positive that we had solved all our warranty issues within the first camping season. Keep in mind we were in the trailer for four months total during that camping season. However, going into our second season in the trailer, we had more issues that surfaced. A few of these issues were complicated and would have been expensive if not for the fact that we were still covered by the manufacturers' warranty.

So the point here is to take real advantage of the warranty period and make sure that you use everything on your travel trailer and that you use it often. Once that warranty period is over, you are on your own. If you are buying a travel trailer for very occasional use, you may be at risk for missing something that could have, and should have, been covered under warranty.

As we mentioned previously, document everything that you find on your warranty punch list. Also, document every conversation you have with your dealership and manufacturer. Document the dates, times, who you talked to, and what was discussed. The more clearly you document your issues the more likely you are to have a positive resolution.

Chapter 17 - When Problems Arise/Warranty And Otherwise

When you encounter a problem with your travel trailer they will typically fall into several different categories.

1. Problems that are covered under warranty.
2. Problems that occur after the warranty period.
3. Problems that may be covered under an extended warranty.

For those problems that are discovered under the warranty period, it is important that you report them immediately to the dealership and manufacturer and document everything regarding your discussions. I typically save all my email correspondence which includes pictures of the issue(s), and all responses.

If after doing this you feel that your dealership is not responsive then it is time to escalate your issues to the manufactures customer service group. Do not take the Dealers word as gospel if you run into a road block on getting something repaired.

For problems that occur after the warranty period, you will be pretty much on your own. However, if you are just outside the warranty period you may be able to get some "good-will" help from your manufacturer. They may opt to help you completely or supply parts for free and you pick up the labor cost.

I think it is always worth a phone call to find out if you can get some relief. From personal experience I can tell you that I have heard of manufacturers helping travel trailer owners to some degree long after the warranty had expired. It doesn't cost anything to ask.

For problems that may be covered under an extended warranty you will want to contact them immediately upon having a problem. They will probably need to authorize the repair before you can have any work done. I'm not a huge fan of extended warranties, but now with all the things that can go wrong in a trailer, they may be worth it. In any event, you need to know what they are going to cover. In most cases they are not going to cover things like water damage. Knowing your specific policy benefits on an extended warranty is key.

Also please remember that you are responsible for many parts of the trailer during the warranty period. I will repeat myself one more time because this point is forgotten so often: It is your responsibility to periodically inspect the roof to make sure that there are no voids in the sealant. If you find voids, you will need to apply sealant or have your dealership perform this repair.

In addition if you have wasps, or other critters damaging your appliances, that is not the manufacturers fault.

One RV owner had the refrigerators external access area full of grass clippings which had been blown up against the trailer as he mowed on a weekly basis. He wasn't aware of this fact and took the travel trailer into the dealership claiming the refrigerator had failed under warranty. Obviously, this was not covered and rightly so.

So what happens if you are still in your warranty period and are getting no satisfaction from the Dealer or Manufacturer over a valid claim? Well then it may be time to contact an attorney that deals in RV related issues. There are many Lawyers that are branching into this practice as more and more consumers are having problems with no resolution.

Chapter 18 - Maintenance And Common Travel Trailer Issues

If you are reading posts on-line about common travel trailer issues, you have probably seen at least some of the items on the following list. They are the most frequent topics that are talked about on a daily basis. In order to prevent these issues from happening you need to be actively maintaining your travel trailer.

Plumbing Issues and Issues with Holding Tanks

Whether it's a simple leak at a sink faucet or a loose P-trap under the sink, almost all plumbing issues can be prevented with at the very least, a yearly inspection.

Most of the sink and drain plumbing is very easy to access. In our trailer we just open the cabinet doors and check all the fittings. Under the shower there is a small access panel that makes checking the shower drain easy. On one of our first trips out with our new travel trailer we found water on the floor and discovered our bathroom sink p-trap had never been tightened down. This resulted in us checking every p-trap and water line in the trailer and surprisingly every p-trap needed to be tightened.

Problems become more complicated if you haven't taken great care to protect your plumbing system in the off-season. You need to do this by blowing out the lines or running RV antifreeze through the water lines (and p-traps) of your trailer. Not taking the appropriate care of your plumbing system in the off-season can add up to huge dollars in repairs. The result can be anything from broken water lines to a broken water pump or broken water heater.

The same rules apply to holding tanks; make sure they are emptied during the off-season. There is no need to add antifreeze to the empty holding tanks. During the camping season make sure you follow a few simple rules:

NEVER leave your black valve open while camping. This will result in a nasty accumulation of waste in your black tank which will eventually lead to plugging your black tank and making it impossible to dump.

ALWAYS use plenty of water when flushing the toilet.

ONLY dump when the black tank is at least 3/4 full. If it's time to break camp and you are under 3/4 full just add water to reach that level. Then follow the black tank dumping with grey tank dumping to clean out the sewer hose out.

Pest Issues

Whether it's ants or mice no one wants critters running around in their travel trailer. Make sure any points where pests can enter your trailer are sealed. More importantly, do not leave food outside your camper when you are camping. When you return home empty all food out of your camper and clean the food areas completely. You should also remove any items that mice could potentially use as bedding material; paper plates, paper towels, etc.

You can also place bait stations around your RV during the off-season and place d-Con inside just in case a rodent ventures inside. **NOTE**: Please be careful using any sort of rodent bait if you have pets – it is poison for them as well. When we have place d-Con in our trailer it has always been under the bed and in one other protected area that was impossible for our dogs to reach.

As a side note, some state parks (and here I am referring to Texas although it may apply to other states as well) have certain ants that have a habit of infesting trailers and are hard to get rid of (the Tawny Crazy Ants and the Argentine Ants for instance). There are some products that can be used to prevent them from getting inside the trailer but I prefer to know which parks are an issue and avoid those campgrounds.

The Infamous Flat Tire

Nothing ruins a vacation faster than being stuck on the side of the road with a tire problem. Blow outs create some very expensive damage, so here are a few tips:

NEVER have your tires under or over inflated. Check them often and make the necessary adjustments.

ALWAYS check tires to make sure they are nail free and have no dry rot. Torque the lug nuts to specification before each trip.

Get a Tire Pressure Monitoring System (TPMS) in order to avoid hundreds of dollars of damage if a blowout should occur. Often times a blowout will destroy the lower trim on a travel trailer. I have even seen the underside of a trailer destroyed by a blowout.

Fully inflate the spare tire before every trip. People tend to neglect the spare tire. A spare tire cover might be a nice decoration on your rear bumper, but a flat spare tire will not be helpful.

Water intrusion Issues

Water intrusion from the roof and windows is the quickest way to ruin your travel trailer. After every trip with your travel trailer, and at least three times per year (or more depending on how you store it or the climate) get on the roof and inspect it for tears or voids in the sealant. Look around every vent, skylight and air conditioner to make sure everything is water tight. I clean my roof after every trip, for us this means at least 6 to 8 times per camping season. I am always on top of the trailer cleaning and inspecting – better safe than sorry! If you are not comfortable getting on the roof you really need to take it somewhere so a cleaning and inspection can be done.

Check the seals around the windows and replace if necessary – the outside seals do shrink so keep an eye on them. Also check anywhere there is silicone and make sure that it is still intact, if not, then re-seal the area.

Battery Failure

A Travel Trailer battery is not cheap; but distilled water is.

NEVER let your battery discharge completely – this will almost always ruin the battery and require you to drop some big dollars on a new one.

ALWAYS check your battery water levels, at the very least a few times per season.

ONLY use distilled water for filling your battery cells.

In the non-camping season, take your battery home and keep it on a trickle charger. Make sure you keep your battery connections clean and free of rust.

Not having a Process

Not having a system for getting the trailer ready for travel is an invitation for an accident. Every year you see stories where a handrail gets torn off, an open skylight gets hit by a branch, stabilizer jacks were not raised high enough, and the list goes on. I've actually seen someone's travel trailer cargo doors flapping in the wind as they drove by us on the highway. I'm lucky because Tammy follows me around while I pack up and then does the final inspection. Make a list if you need to because there is a lot to remember both inside and outside the trailer. An unfastened door or chair will cause a great deal of damage.

Not using the Travel Trailer enough during the warranty period

One thing RV manufacturer's bank on is that you will not use your trailer much before the warranty period expires. Get out in your travel trailer and spend as much time in it as you can before the warranty period is up. Chances are you will come up with a pretty good list of things that need to be repaired. Don't wait until it's too late to find things that really could have been repaired under warranty.

Chapter 19 - Is it worth the effort

Jennifer and Jeff, and our 71 Jayco

I think at this point you are armed with enough information to make your own decision. We have been doing this for over 30 years now and we have never regretted it.

While there is some work involved in maintaining your camper, it is not an overwhelming amount of time. I certainly spend more time during the year mowing my lawn, then taking care of my travel trailer; although it certainly can seem longer when I'm trying to get the bugs off the front cap after a long trip.

If I have one regret, it's that the kids are grown now. It was a fantastic way to travel as a family. There is nothing more convenient than pulling into a wayside and jumping into the trailer for a quick lunch. There is nothing more fulfilling than experiencing new parts of the country for the first time with your kids. To say that traveling with a trailer is a memory maker would be an understatement.

If you are willing to be a little OCD with your travel trailer and you are even slightly handy, I think you will find that having a trailer is worth the effort and a great way to see the country.

To follow us on our travels, visit us at
www.traveltrailernation.com

Visit and like us on Facebook at
www.facebook.com/jpattexas/

Our Travel Trailers Throughout The Years

The 1971 Jayco Jay Wren

A sixteen foot trailer that was able to sleep five people. The dinette converted to a bed, as well as the couch. Over the couch a bunk bed could be dropped for additional sleeping.

Pros: It had its own furnace and small refrigerator. It introduced us to the travel trailer lifestyle.

Cons: No bathroom and no air conditioning. It was very heavy for its size at 5000 lbs.

The 1990 Mallard Sprinter 26FK

The 1990 mallard was a twenty six foot travel trailer and weighed 4240 lbs.

Pros: Separate bunks for kids and bedroom for us. Nice bathroom, large refrigerator, and easy to tow.

Cons: No air conditioning and no awning. The only place to sit inside the trailer was at the dinette.

The 1992 Prowler M-26B

The 1992 Prowler was a twenty six foot travel trailer. It was set up almost identically to that of the 1990 Sprinter. It weighed 4730 lbs.

Pros: This trailer had air conditioning and an awning. The exterior of the trailer had a Teflon siding which was very easy to clean.

Cons: Again, the only place to sit inside the trailer was at the dinette

The 2001 Trail Cruiser

The 2001 Trail Cruiser was a twenty six foot travel trailer. It was incredibly light for its size at 3570 lbs.

Pros: So light it could be towed with a Jeep Cherokee. It had the first couch in any of our travel trailers, which was inside a bump out that hand cranked in and out. A huge wardrobe near the rear bedroom

Cons: The kitchen was in the rear of the trailer next to the door which made it difficult to be in the kitchen with anyone entering or leaving the kitchen.

2007 Coachman Captiva 288FKS

The Coachmen Captiva was thirty five feet long and was relatively light for its size at 4987 lbs.

Pros: Wonderfully large U-Shaped Kitchen with more cabinets than you could ever hope to fill. It has a large amount of counter space, and a built in silverware drawer and tilting trash cabinet.

Cons: A small couch with no end tables. The exterior decals and surface degraded quickly. It was very difficult to maneuver at gas stations.

2015 Jayco 24RBS

This Jayco was a twenty four foot travel trailer that weighed 4460 lbs..

Pros: A well-constructed trailer that was easily towed and maneuvered at gas stations and into camping spots.

Cons: Unrealistically small for our family with two large dogs. We realized after one season that we had over reacted to our thought of downsizing.

2015 Jayco 27RBOK

Another well-constructed trailer that was 31 feet long and weighed 5958 lbs.

Pros: It has large living area, a huge bathroom with a large shower and a lot of bathroom cabinets. Outside it has an outdoor kitchen and plenty of exterior storage.

Cons: The TV was placed so that your head needed to be turned on an angle to watch. No room to walk around the front of the bed. No cabinet for trash.

2017 Grand Design Imagine

This trailer is almost 34 feet in length and weighs 7240 lbs.

Pros: It has a huge residential interior with a kitchen island. It has two AC Units. The living area has two recliners and a large couch. It has a large bedroom with plenty of space to walk around the bed. The Bathroom has two entrances, one from the hallway and one from the bedroom.

Cons: There is no propane line to rear of trailer (I added this). It has no outdoor kitchen. I'm not thrilled with the Schwintek slide system.

Made in the USA
Middletown, DE
20 March 2019